Passive Income

Make Money Online Through Multiple Income Streams: Step By Step Guide To Create Financial Freedom

By Stephen Aldrich

©2016 by Stephen Aldrich. All Rights Reserved.

Alder Publishing

Table of Contents

Introduction

Chapter 1. Niche Selection is Key

Chapter 2. Drop Shipping

Chapter 3. Affiliate Marketing

Chapter 4. Blogging

Chapter 5. Sell an Online Course

Chapter 6. Building an Email List

Chapter 7. Outsourcing

Chapter 8. Kindle Publishing

Conclusion

Introduction

We all want to live a comfortable life, but what if your career options are not providing you with enough income? What if you are struggling to live each month on income that is just not stretching far enough? You are not alone. Millions of people, including myself have had to look for alternative methods to gain income.

The next hurdle is how do you fit the work needed to gain a second income into the time you don't have? You already have a busy life. Perhaps you are a caregiver for someone with an incurable disease? Maybe you have one or more children, who need to be ferried back and forth from one extracurricular activity to another throughout the week?

There are definitely plenty of things that can zap your income and your time. Fitting a part time job, with specific hours needed to concentrate on the work, may not fit your life.

This is where passive income can save you. The IRS categorizes income in three ways: active, passive, and portfolio. Passive income, according to the IRS is rental activity or trade (business) activity. Property income is rental income. All other passive income options are considered trade activity because they deal with business-oriented concepts like drop shipping, affiliate marketing, blogging, kindle publishing, and others.

Not every passive income option is equal. Some of the ways to make income through a business or using online resources are not as effective as they are purported to be. You want to have multiple streams of passive income, with the ability to scale a stream of passive income to $1,000 per month. The $1,000 is a benchmark in passive income that helps you know whether it is worthwhile or not.

If you are working 50 hours a week on what is supposed to be "passive income" and earning $250 that is not worthwhile. When I say $1,000 made from passive income each month, I mean you are literally earning money without actively doing a thing.

Now, it won't happen overnight. The information you will learn here is not a magic solution to your income needs. It takes work to set up your passive income streams and hit the benchmark. Depending on your choice of income streams, you may find some options take more work than others.

The key to passive income is in the marketing end. Anyone can write a book and publish it on Kindle, but not everyone will make money because there are thousands upon thousands of books added each month. The competition can limit how much, if anything you make, even if you choose a niche topic.

I want you to sit for a few minutes before reading on. Write down your expectations for passive income.

Do you have a list?

Look at the list and examine which expectations seem levelheaded and realistic. If you wrote you want to make $1,000 in the first month of starting your passive income, you'll need to re-evaluate your thinking. If you said you can make $1,000 per month after three to six months, then you are looking at the reality of the situation. I'm not saying it can't be done, it's just better to not have high expectations when first starting because it can be that much easier to give up if things don't go as planned.

First, outline what you need to truly make in a month to alleviate any financial troubles you have.

Second, examine where you can find the time to set up your passive income streams.

Third, choose a passive income stream that you are familiar with. Obviously it is best if you chose something you have prior experience with, whether it is selling an eBook based on your degree or learning how to dropship because you understand retail needs.

I know it is difficult to believe in a person writing an eBook, when you do not know if you can trust what they are telling you. So, I'd like to share a little about my knowledge and experience in passive income. For a while, I would try anything that came to my attention.

If people and magazines said you could make thousands each month, taking surveys, I tried it. I would sit down, sign up for the free account, start taking surveys, and earn nothing. Each time I tried something I was told to sign up for this or that before I'd be given a small earning for the surveys, which was never enough to convert to cold hard cash. I was under the impression due to marketing that it would not take more than a few minutes each day, but in reality those who made thousands doing surveys would sit at their computer taking survey after survey for eight to ten hours straight and not care if their email account blew up with junk mail from every company in the world.

Next, I went to a seminar on affiliate marketing and drop shipping. I was told if I invested $3,000 to set up an account I could market any product I wanted, drop ship it, and publish 10 different websites, with different retail goods. All it would take was a few months of setup, marketing, and using peers to help market what I was selling. It worked for some, but I didn't have the money to invest. I needed money—not to put it into something else.

Thus, I started looking into the one marketing skill I had—writing. Creating a blog and eBooks has provided me with the revenue streams I was looking for, with a hobby and a career I enjoyed. Now, I make a living marketing my own work. For the blogs, I allow ads to be placed on my pages that are relevant to the content I create and get paid for those ads. With eBooks, I market topics I am familiar with and reap the rewards. I know I am helping someone with a subject I have knowledge in and I make a difference with words.

So, what can you make a difference with? Where do your talents lie?

- Marketing?
- Retail?
- Writing?
- Emailing?
- Outsourcing?

Whatever you have a knowledge base for and in, you can turn into a passive income stream. It will take time, honesty, and integrity. You never want to make the mistake of providing false advertising to your audience, and you never want to overextend yourself into an audience you do not understand. You'll learn about niche concepts, shortly, and why they are important.

Be thinking about the three steps outlined above, what you wish from your passive income, and what you already know that can be put to use.

Chapter 1: Niche Selection is Key

Do you visit websites that sell more than one related topic? If you stick with the big box retailers like Wal-Mart, Target, and Amazon, then you do. You shop on a website that has just about anything you could need. Yet, there are other large retailers like Barnes and Nobles, Macy's, and JC Penney that have a website to represent what they sell in stores. Big retailers have the mass marketing budget and brand name to make it easy for you to go to their website, buy goods, and return them to a brick and mortar location if you are unsatisfied. The little business trying to make it in the online world has to be more selective.

You need to have a niche if you are going to survive on the internet with a website. Passive income only works when you have a low overhead, low time-consuming project, and they know how to get your products or services sold. Therefore, the key to your success is choosing a proper niche to start selling your products or services in.

Go to your web browser right now. Type in "pets." How many results do you get for that one word? If you used Google as your browser you most likely received local websites first, with about 871,000,000 results total or more for you to scroll through. Let's type in "pets grand rapids." Now the results are only 707,000.

What if you sold only toys and no pet food, what do you think the results would be? If you add "toys" to "pets grand rapids" the results are further reduced to 518,000. We'll type in "pets grand rapids toys Dutch shepherd" next. The results from Google show about 376,000.

As you can see the results displayed are less the more you narrow down the search. However, there are still over three hundred thousand results for such a narrowed search.

Let's do another search. This time type in "FTD dementia." Google shows approximately 253,000 results for this type of dementia. If you tack on "life expectancy" to FTD dementia, the results become 44,700.

You should be understanding the pattern. The broader your keyword search is—the more results you will see. The more narrowed in focus you are, the more narrowed results will appear. Now, the ticket is to understand what your audience is going to do and know.

An older person who rarely spends time on computers is either going to search broad terms or have their younger generations help them. An older person who is retired will muddle through the searches, learning as they go to refine their search. The younger generation is being taught that Google and other search engines are getting better at narrowing down the search. They know if a question is typed into Google, an answer will be found. Ten years ago if you typed a question into Google, you would not get the same refined results.

So, yes, you do need to have a niche and figure out what that niche is based on the popularity of word usage; however, you cannot discount how your audience will think of you and what you have to offer.

There are three big things that you need to account for as you consider what your niche should be, once you decide what you are going to sell.

1. What are you selling?

2. Where are you selling it?

3. Who are you selling it to?

What you are selling will help you determine your niche. Let's take a look at another example: scuba diving.

If you live in Colorado, you may see 39,900,000 results, with the nearest results in the city or town you live in. Let's say you live near Loveland, so you might see the three closest shops to that city. All you did was type in two words, "scuba diving," and the nearest locations popped up.

Your audience may not live in Colorado or be interested in Colorado scuba diving locations. In fact, your audience may be from around the USA and the world looking for diving options in Colorado. For them to find a narrowed result based on what they are interested in, they will need to type in "scuba diving Colorado." Just like you would want to type in "scuba diving

Florida Keys," if you wanted to plan a dive vacation in the Florida Keys.

So, one you need to choose niche keywords based on what you sell, where you want to sell it, and who your audience is going to be. This is why your niche selection is important to your passive income.

What if you were trying to sell pet supplies? You would have millions of other websites to contend with. But, if you are selling scuba diving to your local community, you have fewer competitors. You also have fewer worries when it comes to your keywords and marketing.

To bring niche selection to the forefront, let's go with another example. Put yourself in a horticulturist's shoes. You love plants and grow plants. You want to turn this hobby into a local passive income business. You decide you are going to focus on one plant type because there are billions of plants, but you want to make money.

You set up a website offering information about pineapple plants, you also start YouTube videos, and you use website advertising to make money. For each click your audience makes using an ad on your website you get paid. You have tied your website and YouTube videos to a place that sells pineapple plants locally. So, with each click that sends a person to the place that sells pineapple plants and the customer buys a plant, you make money.

You are able to target your audience, specifically, because they are interested in only one type of plant. Now, it does not mean they didn't buy other things from the site, but your niche allowed them to find you and follow your links, so that you made the money versus trying to capture millions of people interested in billions of different plant species.

Niches can be found in blogging, affiliate marketing, drop shipping, and other passive income options. You do need to search for a niche that will provide you good money. A wrong niche is going to mean less income for you, if any at all. Remember back to the pet example all the way down to the last example. As you were asked to narrow the search, there was less competition to contend with. Yes, people own pets and there are millions who do. But, most of these individuals are going to buy their items in a local store, a warehouse store, or online where the deal is too sweet to pass up. For example, if you have a wholesaler who is willing to offer prices at a discount of 25% off, with no shipping a person will be tempted to purchase their pet supplies online. But, what if you find out the local store offers your pet food at $36.00 and the online website offers their food for $35.00, but unless you spend $100.00, you have to pay $20.00 in shipping? A person might be willing to purchase enough food to make the $100.00; however, what if they only go through a bag of food every three months? The food they purchase could be out of date. These are the kinds of things your audience is thinking.

This is why you need to consider the niche, the competition, and the audience. If you do not, you could choose a great niche in terms of products people buy often, but never make any sales. The right niche is going to be something you can market for enough sales to reach your $1,000 per month goal. You also have to choose something you are familiar with in an area online that is missing a great quality product or service.

What you learned:

- Niche selection is key.

- The niche you choose equals the money you make, so a poor niche means less money.

- You need to consider your competition to lower competitor interference in your passive income money plan.

- You need to decide what you are selling based on the competition.

- You need to keep in mind where you are selling it as a way to narrow or broaden your niche using keywords.

- You also need to consider who you are selling your niche products or services to in order to make the most money.

Don't be greedy. Target the people you know are most interested because they can help build your customer base. If you sell to people who are looking for your products, they will tell their friends about it, and by word of mouth you are going to make more income from your passive income business.

Chapter 2: Drop Shipping

Drop shipping is a great way for you to make passive income, but not without a little effort on your part. Like with most successful passive income revenue streams, they take a good amount of work upfront. Some of them take a ton of work up front and then time-to-time maintenance to keep everything in tune. Drop shipping is no different. You will need to establish a website. Establishing a website includes, buying the domain name for the website, buying hosting so the site is able to go live, and finally either getting a web designer to design the website or designing the theme yourself through something like WordPress and Optimize Press. This website will provide products that you do not store in your home, but buy directly from the warehouse.

You are going to buy your products from a third party, and have it directly shipped to the customer from that third party. You will never see or handle the product. The reason this has a low overhead and low cost to you is due to no inventory. You do not own inventory or have any stock to keep track of. The manufacturer or wholesaler is going to handle the merchandise directly.

With drop shipping, the best way for you to make money is to use a site like Shopify. You are able to connect with wholesalers and manufacturers on the website, as well as gain notice around the world with your site.

Before explaining more about sites like Shopify, let's take a look at the benefits of drop shipping.

- Less capital is needed to start your passive income strategy. With drop shipping, you never buy the goods you sell, so you can launch an ecommerce store with a very small investment. The drop shipping concept allows you to buy as you make sales, thus you will only need to purchase the product right away, if you have already been paid by the customer.

- You can get started very easily since you do not need to pay for or manage a warehouse, pack or ship your orders, track the inventory for accounting purposes, handle returns, or inbound shipments, or continue to manage and order products. All you will really need to pay for is a Shopify account, possibly domain name, and hosting.

- You can run your business from your home office, thus you have minimal overhead. In fact, your computer, internet, phone, fax, and printer are about the only things you will need to spend money on. You will have a little electricity that goes towards your business, but it is minimal. This energy usage is particularly minimal if you are converting time you used to search online to making passive income.

- You can choose a wide selection of products, as long as they fit within your niche. Let's say you are starting an essential oil business. You would want to sell essential oils, bottles to mix essential oils, soap making kits for those who want to use essential oils for soap, and the list can go on. The point is you can choose to sell one product and its related products as a means of making more money. Anytime a supplier lists something on their site for sale, you can upload it to your site.

- You can eventually end up selling your drop shipping "store", aka your website, for thousands of dollars. A few friends of mine have put in the effort and created great drop shipping stores and have grown them over the course of a few years, then they sold them for between $40,000-$60,000. There are others that have sold for much more than that.

There is one caveat to selling multiple vendor items. Your wholesaler or manufacturer may offer many products for several different niches. You may not want to post everything on your website that they offer. What would you think if you came across a site that sells pet food and saw a blockbuster DVD for sale? It would be confusing correct? Now, if the savvy website owner was selling pet DVDs and pet food it would make sense.

So when you choose what products to sell, make certain it is within your niche and not something completely outside of it. If you are going to sell more products than what is in your first chosen niche, you need to start a new website for those products. You can link your two sites and have others link to you, but you definitely need to have two sites or make it very clear that you are more like a "big" box store offering multiple products. This second option takes multiple pages in your menu, with clear distinctions and a good tag line to get people to your site.

It is often more work than multiple sites that are niche based.

- Flexible location is also a part of the drop shipping benefits. Without a need to have your business in a brick and mortar location, you can take your laptop anywhere you have an internet connection and fulfill orders. When an email order comes in, you can select to fill the order from your drop shipper via the internet, and within minutes the drop shipper is going to receive the order and put it in their queue. You will need to communicate with the customer to let them know when the drop shipper is projecting an arrival date. You also need to keep in contact with your suppliers to ensure your orders are being filled on time.

- You can increase your sales, without increasing your time. Once you have established your website and are making sales, it will not matter if you become busier with sales. The drop shippers, you deal with are going to pick up the additional orders, allowing you to expand your business without worry.

As with any business, even those that offer passive income, you have drawbacks.

- You can get started so easily because there are low margins in this business. By low margin, it means it is a highly competitive industry, where you have to sell products at very low prices to gain revenue. If your website is poorly constructed or without decent customer service, you are going to find your profit is destroyed instantly.

- Shipping can be complex. You may offer several products on your website, but they are all from different suppliers. For instance, say you are selling a hard to find book. This book is available through wholesale publishers, used. You have to contact four suppliers to get four copies. The books will not arrive at the same time for the customer, and the shipping will be tallied for each supplier—not just once. If the book is $1.00 from two suppliers who charge media shipping at $3.99, and the other two books are $2.00 with media shipping at $3.99, then the customer is charged 21.96, not

$4.00 for the books and $3.99 for the shipping. It can make a customer hesitant to purchase the items they need; especially, if the competition has one supplier they can purchase all items from.

- Inventory can be an issue. When you stock items you own, you know exactly what you have to sell. With drop shipping, you are depending on the inventory being available or at least accurate on their website. Sometimes syncing your inventory records with wholesalers or manufacturers is not as accurate as you would like.

- Suppliers can also make errors. You get blamed for the errors because you were the face of the supplier, and you also have to accept responsibility. You have to apologize, attempt to correct the mistake or provide the customer with their money back. It damages your reputation versus the suppliers.

At this point, you are probably asking if it is worth it? It is, when you offer drop shipping as a service and not as a role. Manufacturers, wholesalers, and retailers can all act as drop shippers, just like you wish to do. This is why your role is not a part of the supply chain, but as a service to offer a better price than other companies. It takes having the proper arrangement with a legitimate manufacturer or wholesaler. There are lots of companies out there offering wholesale and manufacturer services that are not legitimate, so beware.

How the process works:

A customer is going to place an order online at your website.

You are going to confirm that you received the order.

You will then check with the supplier or suppliers you work with. You will find the best price for the item, including the best shipping option.

If the goods are available, you will send a second email to the customer, letting them know the expected ship date.

When the item is confirmed as shipped by the supplier, you will charge the customer's credit card or PayPal or other account.

The customer will wait for their package, track the package via the wholesaler, and only contact you if their product shows up late, broken, damaged, or otherwise incorrect. The wholesaler or manufacturer is totally anonymous to the end customer. Your logo and return address is on the label. The drop shipping wholesaler only works in stocking and shipping the products. You, the merchant, are responsible for the website, marketing, customer service, and all other areas of the "merchant" business.

Finding Wholesalers

Websites like Shopify do not offer wholesalers or suppliers. They do help you understand how to find these businesses, but they are just a place to host your ecommerce website.

First, let's take a look at how to tell a legitimate wholesaler from a fake one:

- A legitimate wholesaler is not going to ask for any ongoing fee from you. Supplier directories typically ask for a membership fee to help you find suppliers that are legitimate. Otherwise, any supplier asking for a fee is actually not legitimate.

- You will need to apply for a wholesale account. A wholesale account will be at cost to you, so that you can mark up the cost to the customer. Any company that does not offer an approval process for the wholesale account is selling to the general public and typically at inflated prices.

- A standard in the drop shipping industry is a pre-order-fee. This fee is $2 to $5 depending on the company, the complexity of the order, and the size of the order. The reason for the fee is because of the higher cost of shipping a smaller order or single items versus bulk ordered items.

- Some wholesalers will require a minimum initial order size. This is the lowest amount you have to purchase for orders to be filled. You have two options to get around the minimum order size since you do not want a garage full of items. You can offer to put the money in an account as credit. In other words, as you get orders and have them filled the wholesaler or supplier will charge your account. It meets the minimum purchase requirement without you having to store the items. You can also look for suppliers that have a smaller minimum order for the first round.

Now that you have a handle on how to tell wholesalers and suppliers apart. Here is how to find them:

1. Contact the manufacturer of products you want to sell. Explain that you know a lot about their product and would like to have a list of their wholesale distributors in order to sell their products. Some manufacturers may not allow drop shipping. However, most will because it gets more of their products sold.

2. Google is a second option. You can search for wholesale suppliers for X product that you like. Unfortunately, many suppliers do not advertise, and their websites are often poorly created. You will need to search without SEO tactics meaning you want to use

"distributor," "bulk," "warehouse," reseller," and "supplier" in your search to see what comes up for the products you want to sell.

3. Trade shows are another great way to gain notice. You will need a business name and to pay the registration fee for a trade show. Once you establish your business, you can attend the trade show with products you know you want to sell. Speak with the various reps, figure out if they are willing to offer their suppliers and start contacting the suppliers to set up a drop shipping account.

4. Directories are extremely common because of the passive income bug. Directories are built by for profit companies, so you will often need to pay to gain access to the list. You can highlight the suppliers that fit your niche.

A few Suppliers to Check Out

Through Shopify, you can access this list of supplier directories. You will need to pay a fee as they are directories, but they have been well researched:

- Worldwide Brands
- SaleHoo
- Doba
- Wholesale Central

What you Learned:

- You know you need a website
- You need a wholesaler or supplier
- You also learned how to differentiate fake from real suppliers
- You know at least four supplier directories you can look through to contact suppliers

If you decide to go the drop shipping route, there is still more to learn. This is a highlight of your drop shipping passive income option. You also should understand there is a lot of work involved in the beginning portion of setting up a drop shipping business. Just finding the suppliers can take time, once you have decided on a niche. Setting up the website, establishing your integrity, and investing in the technology to communicate with both customers and suppliers will take some investment of money and time.

This path is not for everyone. To get started as a drop shipper you will need:

1. The income to purchase proper technology.
2. Excellent phone skills and customer service.
3. Organization and determination.

4. The time to set up a website, the knowledge of how to make it user friendly, and professional in appearance.

If you need income today, to the tune of $1,000, then setting up a drop shipping ecommerce business in a place like Shopify is not for you. It is for the person that has money to invest, albeit you only need a small amount, and for the person who has the time to market their website. Ecommerce hosts do not do the marketing for you. They offer you professional website themes, mobile ecommerce options, experts to help customize your store, a brand, your own domain, a website builder, blogging platform, and minimal marketing. For example, you will find articles on SEO (search engine optimization), how to create a sitemap, programs to generate codes and coupons, Google AdWords Credits, email marketing apps, product reviews, gift cards, and ways to sell on Facebook. Ecommerce hosts are not going to do the marketing work for you.

It is the marketing where many drop shippers get lost in the competition, not the prices or the look of their website, but in actually getting clients to their site.

Think carefully if you have the time, skills, and a desire to try drop shipping.

Chapter 3: Affiliate Marketing

Affiliate marketing has quite a few myths about it. This can lead to a misunderstanding that all affiliate marketing is a pyramid scheme, where you don't make money, but the person at the top does. Affiliate marketing is a commission-based program, so there are going to be individuals making more commissions than you because they have established their plan years ago.

Defining Affiliate Marketing

Affiliate marketing is about selling products, but not products you invested your time and money into creating. Affiliate marketing is about selling a product you believe in via a platform. It is a product already in existence. You might think this sounds an awful lot like drop shipping, and to a degree it is. There is one major difference—you usually have the product available and send it rather than drop shipping it, but you can also do both.

You can be an affiliate marketer who drop ships a product for a specific company.

The benefits:

- You earn a commission instead of a full fee.

- The company you work for has the product and you sell for them, not a wholesaler or numerous suppliers.

- Customers benefit because you provide a product they need or desire.

You will want to start off with a product you are extremely familiar with. You should not recommend something you don't use or have never seen. If you cannot be confident about the product you are selling, then you will have a hard time promoting it on your site, through blogs, and using other marketing procedures.

You also do not want to tell anyone to buy a product when you are an affiliate marketer. Recommending products are important. You have to provide validity and integrity for what you do—it separates you from a pyramid scheme by being honest, forthright, and truly selling something you believe in. If you don't have experience with the product—how can you tell someone else to buy it? Pushing someone to buy something is also not going to help you make money. If anything they will run away versus make a purchase. People want recommendations and reviews, not hard sales.

The idea behind affiliate marketing is that a company with a product has numerous websites online marketing their product. They do not have to spend as much on their own marketing because they have individuals like you doing their work. You gain commissions each time a product is sold, but not if someone follows your lead and only spends a few seconds on the website. There are schemes out there that offer cost per action or CPA payments, as well as cost per click or cost per mile (CPM is an estimated payment based on views of the website). Most companies are more apt to offer a payment for a sale versus these other options because someone can get millions of views without making a sale. It's because too costly to offer a cost per click.

How Affiliate Marketing Works

Affiliate marketing works in different ways based on how the company you are working with is set up. Some affiliate marketing programs have a tier structure, which is how the myth of a pyramid scheme got started. The first person to offer affiliate marketing is usually the company, they reap the most from the sales. They hire and offer a deal to a person like you, who signs up for a specific commission amount based on sales. When you make a sale, you earn a piece of the pie from the sale of the goods. Your piece of that sale is larger than affiliate marketer B and C. B signed up after you and under your company code. They help you market the products with their own website. C also has a website. Both B and C will make the same commission. If they get someone to sign up with their code, then they split a piece of the sales, earn a higher amount than their sign up marketers, and still earn less than you do for the sales.

Since the idea is about the more advertising there is online through e-mail marketing, pop-up ads, contextual advertising, and web banners, the more products a company can sell, companies work hard to find hundreds of affiliate marketers. You really can earn a commission off of an affiliate product through so any ways. Having an email list to promote product offers, having a youtube channel where you can link affiliate products that you use and recommend under each video, having a social media following, it goes on and on.

It creates stiff competition. It is also the reason that you want to find a deal that offers a high commission based on the industry calculation for pay. If you can get paid for cost per mile or cost per click versus cost per sales, then you will be paid more just for sending someone to your site or the company's website.

Some great websites where you can find plenty of physical and online products to earn affiliate commissions off of are Amazon and Clickbank. Actually Amazon has a policy where if you promote an affiliate product for them and someone clicks on that product and does not buy it, but ends up buying anything else off Amazon within a certain time frame, you will earn an affiliate commission off those products.

Another great way to find affiliate products is to just search various niche websites and scroll to the bottom and see if they have an affiliate program.

The Disadvantage of Affiliate Marketing

When you start out, you need to build a website or some type of email list or following. This website will host products you want to sell. It is also a website that looks exactly like other marketers doing the same thing. Yes, you can individualize these sites a little, but in general, when you purchase the option to be an affiliate marketer, your site looks like dozens of others.

Your prices may reflect some differences, such as coupon deals or free shipping that you offer. If you offer free shipping or discounts, it is often based on your commission. You may end up making 10 cents per sale, but if you have millions of sales, you are making decent money. If you don't offer free shipping or discount deals and make $3 per sale, but only sell 10 items you are making less.

So, one you have to have a better way to get the customer to buy from your website versus another affiliate marketer. If you sign up for a program that offers you a commission each time you get someone to sign up for affiliate marketing, as well as sales, then you can make money in two ways.

The other thing about affiliate marketing is that you need to be savvy in sales and marketing. If you don't know anything about marketing or know you have a hard time marketing products, then you will have a difficult time sticking with this option.

Affiliate marketing requires a lot of time when you first set it up. Once you have established customers, you need to continue to blog and send out emails. A great way to do this is to send an email that offers the return customer a deal, but also a deal for their friends.

For example:

We noticed it has been three months since you ordered X product. We have a two for one deal going on right now. As an added bonus tell a friend about us and they will receive 10% off their first purchase.

Now, you have gotten the return customer to make another purchase and potentially gained a new customer. Word of mouth via your current customers is one of the best affiliate marketing secrets out there. But, it takes time and the right message.

What you Learned:

- Affiliate marketing is about cost per sales, cost per clicks, or cost per action based on selling a product for another company.

- You are the marketer who has to generate leads to your website in order to make a commission on the sales.

- It takes time to set up your website, money to begin the process, and time to create new advertisements.

- Once your site is established, you still need to spend a few hours on key sales days, to generate new marketing campaigns.

- Then, you sit back and let the sales come in.

- Each week you need to create a new marketing campaign to launch just prior to the busiest online sales times.

Studies have proven when people are home and surfing the internet. For affiliate marketing to work, you need new marketing campaigns that launch at the times your target audience will be online.

Affiliate marketing is a great option once you get it established. It will always take belief in the product you sell, time to set up a campaign, and marketing knowledge. Affiliate marketing is not for everyone. It can also be paired with drop shipping and other passive income stream choices as a way to reach your benchmark $1,000 per month. If you dream of sitting on a beach with a computer making money, while sipping cocktails, it's possible, once you establish a proper marketing website and customer base. Often it takes three months to a few years based on the products you choose to market and how successful your marketing campaigns are.

Chapter 4: Blogging

Blogging is a cost effective way to market products you sell, services you offer, or information you like discussing. Most people might think that blogs are free and they make no money, but those who have made a life through passive income know differently. Blogging is a way to make passive income and to strengthen other passive income streams.

There are certain rules for setting up a blog to make money from it. Anyone can set up a free blog, but you don't have control over how advertisers use your site. Sure, you are sharing your ideas, but you are not actually making money.

The first thing you need to do is ignore the "free" options. WordPress.com is one of the most well-known blogging sites; however, if you sign up for their free option you will have a .wordpress.com domain. You will also be subject to any advertisement the site wishes to put on your website. Also when you chose a free domain the domain doesn't truly belong to you. You do not want to build up a great blog and then have something happen to it because of a change in wordpress' terms or for whatever reason. When you buy a domain and hosting you truly own the site and it is there to stay for as long as the internet is around.

You need a blog site that you can control. WordPress sells blog sites. There are three options, one with more control for big brand businesses and one for the average passive income person like you, and another for personal blogs. You can also find others, but if you truly want to set up a blog with minimal cost and no fuss, WordPress.com is the best option out there.

The personal blog package provides a custom domain name, SEO features, email and live chat support, free themes, design customization, 3GB of storage space, and the ability to remove WordPress.com ads. It is not for making money.

To make money with your blog, you need to at least have a premium account, which is $8.25 per month, billed yearly. With this account, you receive advanced design customization, 13 GB of storage, and the ability to monetize your site. Monetizing your site means you get to add advertising to your site through the WordAds program and gain money from the impressions.

If you spend $24.95 per month, billed annually, you gain advanced SEO, Google Analytics, and the ability to remove WordPress.com branding, not just the ads. Your brand will be the center of the focus. The idea is to give you more options to make your brand the center of attention, while still making money from the impressions.

An impression is a view or ad view that leads the visitor to a displayed web page. The number of impressions you get from an advertisement is based on how many times a particular page loads. If you have an advertisement on your blog that sends a reader to an affiliate website, you earn money. You are earning that money from the company posting the ad on your website. This is the reason you want to have control over the ads that appear on your blog site.

If you do not have the control, then you are not monetizing your ad space, so someone is making money by posting ads on your blog, but you are not getting a cut of that money.

You don't have to spend $300 per year to monetize your blog. It helps because you get to monetize your blog with ads, as well as make sure your brand is the only one on the site.

However, just starting out, with a small passive income stream, you can begin with a simple site that allows you to control the ads.

How to Set Up a Blog

Millions of blogs are out there. Remember the discussion on finding a niche? You need your blog to serve a need that will gain attention. You have to find the 1% topic that everyone else is overlooking. It is tougher now than when people started blogging more than two years ago.

But, don't worry, you can find a topic. You just have to think outside of the box. You may already have something from your personal life that provide you a unique experience. For example, going through the loss of a loved with that suffered dementia has given me a unique perspective. Discussing topics that scientific sites and the ALZ organization doesn't touch is easy.

It is what you do once you find a topic in a niche that can make blogging a little difficult.

1. You need to meet a need.
2. Discover who your target audience is.
3. Ensure your readers can depend on you.
4. Diversify.
5. Be disciplined.
6. Find and support advertisers.
7. Have an IT back up.

The topic you decide on should help you narrow down your target. Going with the dementia topic, there are more than two types of dementia. There is a pseudo-dementia that comes from underactive or overactive thyroid, FTD, Alzheimer's, vascular dementia, mixed dementia, and the list goes on. Each of these dementias will have a different target audience because a family member who is acting as a caregiver needs to know about their family member's type of dementia. It is the same as a person who owns a Dutch Shepherd. They want information on their dog breed, not mixed dog breeds or small dog breeds like wiener dogs.

The hard part comes in when you need to help your readers believe in you. First, get rid of the idea that you can create the perfect blog without mistakes. Everyone makes a mistake now and then. It is difficult to catch every grammatical mistake, even with the help of editors and editing software. Just look at the NY Bestsellers list, choose a book, and if you look hard enough, you will spot a grammatical mistake. The truth is—the people who are going to notice these are English professionals and those who tend towards analyzing everything to a tee. Most of your audience is a hard working group who wants to read about a topic, is not looking closely for errors, and will trust in your information if it is reliable.

This doesn't mean you should only spend 5 minutes on a blog and upload it. You still want to strive for perfection, but don't worry if you miss something and find it later or have someone point it out.

When discussing reliability, it is about providing information that is correct. For example, if you are creating an entertainment website about local places, you don't want to be wrong or unreliable. If you tell someone to eat at a restaurant, then you better be honest about that restaurant. You need to provide the proper pricing for food, such as appetizers being between $6 and $12, meals being $12 to $20, etc. You also need to be honest.

If I were to write a review about a local restaurant I like to go to, I would tell the readers I know the owners. I would tell them what I like and do not like about the food choices. I would also be honest about any issues I've had. For example, I would warn them about one of the servers who is never friendly, but still has a job at that restaurant. I'd tell the reader not to be put off by that one server because everyone else, including the owners is great at customer service. They also know there is an issue with that server. You have to look passed the server to enjoy the amazing onion rings, pizza, salad wedges, and awesome hamburgers. The ambience is also wonderful because it is on a river, with plenty of nature to observe.

You can see the point I am trying to make. I'm sharing the benefits, letting people know, I know the owners, and being honest about one bad server. If I didn't mention the server or failed to mention that I know the people who own the place, I'd be doing a disservice to the reader. It is also a way to establish trust in what I talk about. A reader is more apt to trust me the next time if I was honest about my review versus leaving the important details out.

Let's say you are using your blog to help sell the eBooks you are an affiliate marketer for. You need to be honest about your reviews of these books. You also need to let people know that you are making money when they purchase a book. It would be like saying, "hey buy this $300 textbook that I hated," if you were not honest.

You are going to be associated with your brand. Do you want hundreds of hate websites to pop up about you or worse be accosted on the street by someone who recognizes you and your blog? Of course not. You want to earn money; thus you need to be reliable.

Diversification is necessary because you cannot just make money from advertisers. Many people who own a blog also use affiliate marketing. They allow ads to be posted on their website, but then sell products through affiliate marketing sites. Their blog is actually a marketing tool for those sales.

The key to making money and keeping your readership is to be disciplined in when you post. You need to religiously post at the same time each week, every few days, or each day. If you have something to say or review, you might provide a blog post each day. However, most people have two to three posts a week.

You need new content for SEO purposes, but also to help remind readers that you are still online and have valuable information for them.

Also make sure you have an IT option should your home internet or computer breakdown or stop working for a short time. You never want to be late with your post. If necessary, write a post and set it to upload automatically at a certain time of day, on a certain day. This is possible.

Finding Advertisers

It is fairly easy to find advertisers, but do you want everyone you find? No. You want to be relied on. To be reliable, you need to have ads your target audience is interested in and have advertisers you trust. You can be approached by numerous people asking to post ads on your site, but you are not going to choose everyone that asks. You are also going to search for advertisers, but again, you will only choose advertisements you can trust. If you trust them, then you know your readers can. It will limit the money you make, but on the other hand, you want to make passive income without having to redo your advertising arrangements because your reputation has been blown.

What you Learned:

1. You need to set up a blog website that lets you control the ads.

2. Your blog can be about information, services, or products.

3. You can tie your blog to an affiliate marketing scheme to make two income streams.

4. You can use ads to make money.

5. Ads need to be to reliable websites that will not hurt your reliability and integrity.

Above all, if you are going to choose a blog, you do need to have a knack for writing. Yes, while one or two grammatical mistakes occasionally is not an issue, you cannot let each blog have errors. You also cannot have errors in the information, product information, or services that you sell occur.

Chapter 5: Sell an Online Course

Selling online courses is another option for passive income streams. There are two ways you can do this: write an online course and market it or market online courses written by other people. There are advantages to selling online courses. You believe in the education of others and wish to help them gain new materials that will help them gain what they require. However, the disadvantage is that you can go terribly wrong when creating content or selling online courses from other sources. You can provide improper information if you are not careful.

- You never want to sell an online course, you write, if you are not an expert in the topic.

- When selling online courses that others write, you need to check their expertise. What is their degree? Have you seen their diploma? Have you read any of their work?

You never want to sell anything you cannot validate. This is why you need to choose online courses to sell that you actually have knowledge about.

How to Sell Online Courses

- Choose valuable content.

- Identify the audience you hope to sell to.

- Visit forums where your target audience will hang out. If necessary, rewrite your course based on what you learn from these forums. Sometimes people complain that they are not learning what they feel is important or they don't understand a concept and wish for more explanation in a simpler manner.

- Market your material based on the target audience you hope to sell to.

- Choose a niche.

- Offer a hook to get your audience's attention, such as time saving tips and tricks for Office Programs.

- Have more than one course that fits the learning needs. You want a series of courses on offer, where the person finishes one course and wants to take the more advanced course. Your plan is to sell a series of courses to one customer versus one course to multiple courses. Return customers will help you gain their friends.

- Choose a platform to sell on. It needs to be one that will confirm appropriate standards for your online courses. To provide validity for your course, you need the SCORM standards. Udemy is just one location that has a free open-source learning management system that provides standards that allow people to trust in your courses. Another option is jvzoo.

- You are going to need a dedicated website for online learning courses you sell. You want to have a catalog and shopping cart that ensures buyers can quickly and effectively purchase your courses.

- Tie your website to a blog where you can share relevant content, as well as make money from the advertisements on that blog site.

- Social media, including Facebook, LinkedIn, Instagram, and Twitter accounts are necessary. You can publish articles, discuss what you sell, and help get your audience engaged and to your online course website.

- Use online search engine indexes to get your courses noticed. Try offering affiliate marketing as a way to get your courses noticed.

- Once you sell a course, stay in contact with your learners. Figure out what they liked, would like improved, and what else they need. A great review can help you sell more courses. It also shows that you care about what they are learning and you want to ensure they are getting what is required.

Selling online courses once you have established your reputation is about keeping up with the content, making sure it is updated when new information is discovered, and marketing it. It is the marketing part of selling online courses that will take the most time, unless you are writing your own courses.

You can make money whenever someone buys your product or a series of your products. You can make money on the advertising and affiliate marketing set up you create.

What you Learned:

- Selling online courses is about reputable content.

- You can write it or hire a writer.

- You can sell as an affiliate for someone who has trustworthy content.

- You earn money through affiliate marketing, advertising, and selling courses.

- It is passive income because once established, you only need to update content, provide new courses, and blog/use social media to hype what you offer.

Chapter 6: Building an Email List

Email lists are another way to make money. The key to email lists is not to sell them for profit, but to use your email list to sell products, services, or information you have. Years ago, it was okay to sell email lists to interested parties. Now, it is aggravating, leads to scams, spam, and while not illegal frowned upon. Why mess with potential income streams just to generate email lists and sell them, when you can make more from keeping your customers happy.

If you are going to generate email lists for sale, then you need to be transparent about it and let your customers know why you are selling the lists. For example, you might garner a list of suppliers and email lists to help affiliate marketers or drop shippers find companies offering the services these individuals need.

Given the trouble building and selling lists can make, the focus from here on out will be about how to build the list using opt in options, landing pages, email autoresponder, and then how you can profit from the list.

Email lists can be very important tools for businesses to use in conjunction with other passive income methods. The idea is for you to build a list of customers, build on that list from customer's friends, social media sites, and other locations.

Here is how you can build an email list:

- Create remarkable email content that will get someone's attention. Often times this is referred to as writing "sales copy". The content needs to be something you would truly share with your friends, without being considered spamming them. People like your friends and family can make purchases from your site or at least help you gain leads from other people. The idea is that the people who subscribe to your emails are going to forward them via email or something like facebook, to friends, colleagues, family, and other people they know, so you get more income from the emails.

- You want to keep your current subscribers updated and sharing information, so you have to include things like social sharing buttons and email to a friend buttons.

- You always need your email list to be optional. So, while you want to share it with your own friends, make sure you send it on to these friends and family with a request, such as "can you look through this and see if it would get your attention." Let your friends know you need help in building your opt-in email list. More often than not they will help if it is a worthy cause. Don't forget those closest to you can help. But, don't rely just on them. You still need to target your main consumer with an opt-in option.

- Promote online contests, so people have to sign up for the contest and give you an email address. Make sure you are not spamming the email account. Let the person see a welcome email, with new deals, and explain the details of the contest. Ask them to opt-in again if they wish to receive more than just communication about the contest coming up.

- Have more than one email subscription option. You want to have targeted content for the audience you hope to turn into customers. This means you need to include things your customers have already bought or would be most interested in, from the pages they already viewed when they sign up for your email.

- You do not want to over-send emails, so only send campaigns out when you truly have something to share. For example, if you do a newsletter each month send it out with a call to action. In the middle of the month send out coupons or a contest offer.

- Every once in a while, send out an email with an opt-in response. Sometimes people forget you exist until you have great offers for them. By sending an email with a request to help you update your email, as well as a coupon to use you will get them to make a purchase.

- A great way to build a huge email list is through putting a little side bar on your blog website where people can click "subscribe" and they will be prompted to enter their email address to gain exclusive content from you or some type of giveaway.

For email lists you have a couple of options for how to send the emails. You want to generate an email in an autoresponder that lets the person know you received their opt-in request, gives them a deal, and gets them back to your site. You also want to use email opt-in on various landing pages to help customers sign up. The worst thing you can do is make this a pop-up. Instead, make it obvious at the bottom or top of the page. Something like, "sign up to get a 20% coupon off your first purchase." Aweber is a great auto responder that you can use to get emails out to your target audience.

The reason you should use an email program is to not only auto respond to your customers, but also to generate emails on a specific day that will be sent out at a time of your choosing.

When you have an email sent out on a Sunday, but you made the email on the previous Monday, you don't have to work on Sunday just to earn money. The point is you want a passive income stream that takes little time, so the more you set up to send out at a different time the better. You could even draft 10 emails all in one day and have them sent out throughout the next two months.

What you Learned:

- Email lists are to help generate income, but not a separate entity.

- You are going to use email list generation with a website you run, whether it is a blog, affiliate marketing site, or drop shipping website.

- Money is made from the follow through or call to action that is used for the customer to make a purchase.

- Never spam anyone.

- Make the emails important to your audience, not what you wish to send to generate leads. Too many emails will make the person opt-out just as quickly as they signed up.

- Keep the deals real. Never put out an email with an incorrect offer or something you are not going to honor.

Chapter 7: Outsourcing

You might be wondering what outsourcing is and how you can make this your passive income scheme. After all, isn't outsourcing something huge corporations do to get talent from countries offering cheaper labor? In this case, you would not be correct. You can actually outsource tasks or work with a third-party as a business instead of being an employee for a corporation. You are going to get a helper to do work for you.

Let's consider the world of eBook publishing, which will also be discussed in the next chapter. There are several writers out there that outsource their talents to companies who are actually outsourcing work to these writers from the companies they work for or work with.

Company A starts off with an eBook they want to publish. They contact a middle person. This middle person has a list of writers who have different sets of expertise. The writer with the best knowledge for the new project is given the work. Company A pays the outsourcing person a fee. The writer earns a percentage of the payment made to the outsourcing person, not the whole amount the company has paid. It is like a commission that the person earns for outsourcing. They find the work and send the work to the one with the talent.

Company A outsources because they can get the work accomplished at a faster rate by bringing someone else in for a specific project. They also get the work accomplished at a lower rate. The work is also something that does not need constant supervision and a lot of the time since the person who conducts the outsourced work needs to maintain clients the work is of better quality.

There are several ways you can begin outsourcing. You can own a company and hire a person to do the work for you.

For example, let's say you have an affiliate marketing website. You don't want to come up with the social media campaigns, email lists, and other work because you don't have experience. You search and find someone willing to do the work for you for a flat rate. You pay that rate, but as you use the campaigns you are generating money from the leads generated.

You can also be the middle person between the company with the work and the talent that can actually get the work done.

The other option is to work harder by outsourcing your talents to various companies. You still have to do the work, but it is something you enjoy. This is less of a passive income option, though.

You are better off sticking with having a website like drop shipping, affiliate marketing, or eBook publishing, where you hire the work done and reap the benefits of continued sales.

For people who already own businesses, outsourcing is a way to scale your business to a larger size without getting inundated with the marketing strategies and other work that needs to be done. You get to use your time more efficiently, thus you get to work on creating various income streams that help benefit everyone.

The more money you can make, the more other employees or contract employees get to make too. If you think of outsourcing like this, then you know that you have the time to get your business to the next level with minimal impact on your time.

What you Learned:

- Outsourcing is about finding new talent.
- You are using outsourcing to find ways to maximize your time.
- You are left with more time to find new income.
- You have a pool of talent that you may not have had before.
- You save money by outsourcing.
- You can also generate more money from outsourcing by gaining more leads.

Sometimes you don't have the time or the talent for certain areas of business. There are also times you just want to focus on what you love. Outsourcing is a great way to make this happen. What if you owned a bookstore, but you were always dragged down by the paperwork, new orders, and the day to day running of the place, rather than getting time to see the books, read the books, and hear from customers? Wouldn't it be more fun to do what you love in your business? You can with outsourcing the things you don't like to do, even hiring a virtual assistant to get the accounting and other paperwork out of the way.

Chapter 8: Kindle Publishing

Outsourcing is one of the ways many of the books are getting published through Kindle. There are writers who are not confident enough to publish under their own name, do not have the savings to publish and market their books, or simply want to focus on the writing versus the marketing of books.

Writers are hired to ghostwrite various topics. They may have a special niche that they deal with or a vast knowledge that allows the writer to discuss more than one topic. Savvy writers choose concepts they consider themselves experts in, as a way to offer validity of the products they are hired to create.

A publishing company may contact a pool of writers directly. They will create a writer's persona and have the writer create the product based on an outline or a title heading. The writer will get a flat rate with no potential to earn royalties from the book sales.

The publishing company or person is the one that receives the royalties. Sometimes there is a middle person who gets work from the publisher, passes it on to their pool of writers, and makes passive income from simply getting the completed book back to the publishing company.

Kindle allows anyone to publish a book. Quality is not always the best because Kindle doesn't check, with as much scrutiny, as other eBook publishing sites. There are certain things that Kindle looks for, such as sensitive topics like inappropriate photos, fowl language, broken grammar, etc. Other than that, nearly anything can be published.

All you have to do is set up an account with Amazon, in their KDP department. It is free to set up a publishing account. When you set up the account, you gain access to free tutorials on how to publish, the template you need to use, and the various options for making money from the published book. You also gain access to emails that help you see what is hot or trending right now. Furthermore, Amazon will help you get book covers from a pool of template images. When the book is published you can choose to make it exclusive to Kindle, meaning you will not publish the book elsewhere. This helps you gain a higher royalty amount. You can also opt to sell it in multiple locations to garner more customers and make less on the royalties at these various publishing locations.

How to Make It Work for You:

As you can imagine there are certain ways for you to make more money from Kindle publishing than others.

You can write the book.

Upload it.

Marketing it.

Your other option is to pay a flat rate to a writer, so they get the time consuming work of researching the topic, writing the book, and editing it. Then, you reap the rewards of uploading it and marketing it.

The money is truly in where and how you market the book.

Marketing with Kindle Publishing

One of the great things about Kindle is that they do market your book for you. However, you have hundreds of books being written each month, on similar topics, so even Kindle cannot market each book with the same success.

You want to take advantage of what they will do to market the book, but also have your own methods.

- Use email lists
- Set up affiliate marketing sites
- Create a blog

- Use social media

The email list option that was discussed in a previous chapter will help you garner people that are more interested in the books you are selling. Of course, they have to buy or read your book first.

The key here is to offer your book for a limited time at a "free to read" price. This is where you put it in the Kindle Unlimited option for free. Someone sees the topic because they are interested in it, reads it, and then opts-in to read more books when you publish a new one.

When you have readers through Kindle Unlimited or offer the book for free for a short time, you want these individuals to leave a review. You should ask in the email or at the end of the book for a review. You don't have to be obvious about it, but ask the person to let others know how much the reader appreciated the content.

Obviously, you want more positive reviews than negative reviews. If there are issues with your book a rewrite to correct them should be made, so that you are selling a quality product.

Using affiliate marketing sites, you can create multiple online websites selling the books or at least products related to the books' topics. For example, if you grow pineapples, set up a website to sell pineapples. Post that you have books on how to grow, care, and repot pineapples available on Kindle. An interested customer will click through to your Amazon site and purchase the book. You have just made a sale to them for a pineapple plant and a book. Now you have two sources making you passive income.

You will always need a blog. When a new book comes out, you will use a press release or a book review by a customer to post on the blog. Readers flock to the blog, follow the link, and buy the book. The link they follow is, of course, an ad for that book.

Social media outlets are also ways to let people know that you have a book available to read. You can use your friends, family (with permission, of course), as well as anyone who stops by your social media websites.

What you Learned:

- Kindle publishing is something you can use in conjunction with other passive income streams.

- You can have books written for you and gain royalties from the sales.

- Kindle publishing requires savvy marketing to make money because it is in the marketing that gets the book noticed by consumers.

- Kindle does help with marketing, but you still need your own campaigns.

Conclusion

Passive income is a real thing. It is not a myth and not something you should consider as a pyramid scheme. You have learned a great deal about many of the best passive income streams you can choose to do, as well as how you can combine the different options to increase your overall income.

Now, you need to choose what you think is going to be the best option for your situation. What do you have the time for? What skills do you have that will fit the passive income schemes available?

Once you know what you are dedicated and determined to do, you can start to slowly early $1,000 per month in extra income. Yes, it will take time. Some people strike the right marketing trick right away and keep up the momentum for years. Others have a slow, but steady start eventually making $1,000 per month after a year of building their online clientele.

You don't have to be one or the other. You simply need to take the information provided and see what you can do. Your life is different from every person who is trying to make passive income. You have different, unique experiences that might provide you with a new revenue avenue.

It is my experience as a writer, blogger, entrepreneur, and someone who has had hands on experience with making money online, it has given me an edge in certain topics over others. Find what you know and are an expert in to make your money. You can do this.

Just remember it takes time, effort, and in time you will make money with little effort because all you will need is to write a new blog, send out a new email campaign or generate new leads via social media.

If you enjoyed this book and feel inclined to leave a review, please do so! Honest Feedback is always welcomed!

www.ingramcontent.com/pod-product-compliance
Lightning Source LLC
Chambersburg PA
CBHW061219180526
45170CB00003B/1063